NATIVE
AMERICAN
NATIONS

THE BLACKFEET

BY BETTY MARCKS

CONSULTANT: TIM TOPPER,
CHEYENNE RIVER SIOUX

BLASTOFF!
DISCOVERY

BELLWETHER MEDIA • MINNEAPOLIS, MN

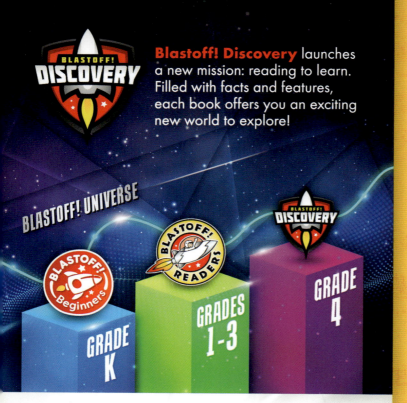

Author's Statement of Positionality:
I am a white woman of European descent. As such, I can claim no direct lived experience of being a Native American. In writing this book, however, I have tried to be an ally by relying on sources by Native American writers and authors whenever possible and have worked to let their voices guide its content.

This edition first published in 2024 by Bellwether Media, Inc.

No part of this publication may be reproduced in whole or in part without written permission of the publisher.
For information regarding permission, write to Bellwether Media, Inc.,
Attention: Permissions Department,
6012 Blue Circle Drive, Minnetonka, MN 55343.

Library of Congress Cataloging-in-Publication Data

Names: Marcks, Betty, author.
Title: The Blackfeet / by Betty Marcks.
Description: Minneapolis, MN : Bellwether Media, Inc., 2024. | Series: Blastoff! discovery, Native American nations | Includes bibliographical references and index. | Audience: Ages 7-13 | Audience: Grades 4-6 | Summary: "Engaging images accompany information about the Blackfeet. The combination of high-interest subject matter and narrative text is intended for students in grades 3 through 8" – Provided by publisher.
Identifiers: LCCN 2023023098 (print) | LCCN 2023023099 (ebook) | ISBN 9798886874402 (library binding) | ISBN 9798886876284 (ebook)
Subjects: LCSH: Siksika Indians–Juvenile literature.
Classification: LCC E99.S54 M13 2024 (print) | LCC E99.S54 (ebook) | DDC 305.897/352–dc23/eng/20230606
LC record available at https://lccn.loc.gov/2023023098
LC ebook record available at https://lccn.loc.gov/2023023099

Text copyright © 2024 by Bellwether Media, Inc. BLASTOFF! DISCOVERY and associated logos are trademarks and/or registered trademarks of Bellwether Media, Inc.

Editor: Elizabeth Neuenfeldt   Series Designer: Andrea Schneider
Book Designer: Laura Sowers

Printed in the United States of America, North Mankato, MN.

TABLE OF CONTENTS

THE CHILDREN OF THE PLAINS	4
TRADITIONAL BLACKFEET LIFE	6
EUROPEAN CONTACT	12
LIFE TODAY	16
CONTINUING TRADITIONS	20
FIGHT TODAY, BRIGHT TOMORROW	24
TIMELINE	28
GLOSSARY	30
TO LEARN MORE	31
INDEX	32

THE CHILDREN OF THE PLAINS

The Blackfeet is a Native American **confederacy** of four nations. The nations include the Amskapi Piikani Nation, the Piikani Nation, the Siksika Nation, and the Kainai Nation. Their homeland stretched across the southern Canadian **provinces** of Alberta and Saskatchewan. It also spanned Montana and North Dakota in the United States. Their **territory** included parts of the Rocky Mountains and the **Great Plains**.

The Blackfeet call themselves *Siksikai'tsitapi*, or "the Children of the Plains." The name "Blackfeet" or "Blackfoot" likely came from the black color of their moccasins. These shoes were often painted with ashes.

NATION NAMES

The Piikani, Siksika, and Kainai Nations are often called "the Blackfoot." But the Amskapi Piikani Nation in Montana is often called "the Blackfeet."

TRADITIONAL BLACKFEET LIFE

ILLUSTRATION OF A BISON HUNT

Blackfeet **culture** and **traditions** are centered around bison. Bison are a **sacred** gift from the Creator. In the past, the Blackfeet relied on bison. They often moved with herds. Men usually hunted using spears and bows and arrows. Over time, some groups drove small herds over cliffs. These bison jumps were called *pishkuns*.

Bison made up most of the Blackfeet diet. The Blackfeet ate fresh meat in summer. Dried meat was often mixed with fat and dried berries. This made pemmican. The Blackfeet also gathered foods such as roots, berries, and eggs.

LIFE BEFORE HORSES

The Blackfeet used dogs to pull their belongings from camp to camp before they got horses. They were called *imataa manistsi* or Blackfeet Dog Travois.

BLACKFEET RESOURCES

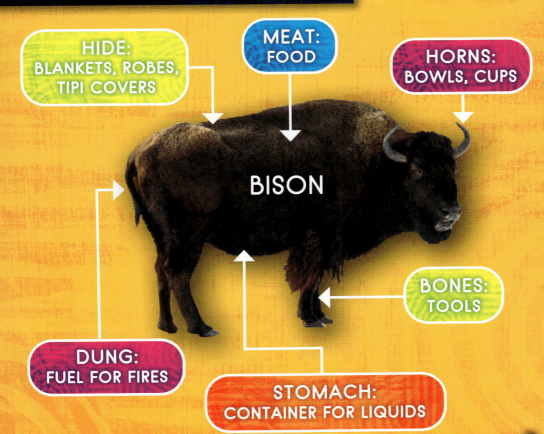

- **HIDE:** BLANKETS, ROBES, TIPI COVERS
- **MEAT:** FOOD
- **HORNS:** BOWLS, CUPS
- **BONES:** TOOLS
- **DUNG:** FUEL FOR FIRES
- **STOMACH:** CONTAINER FOR LIQUIDS

BISON

Early Blackfeet traveled in **bands**. Bands often lived in camps near rivers in winter. Camps were usually close to each other. The close distance kept them safe from enemies. It also allowed bands to share supplies.

People lived in tipis. They were made from wooden poles and bison skins. They were warm during winters and cool in summers. Tipis were quick to put up and take down. This allowed the Blackfeet to follow bison herds with ease.

The Blackfeet were known as fierce warriors. They often fought enemies. Their greatest enemy was the Cree. They also tried to defeat other Plains Nations.

Warriors completed certain acts to grow in rank. Some acts included stealing horses or guns. Warriors who proved their bravery could become War Chiefs. War Chiefs had to continue to prove their ability to remain as Chief.

A Peace Chief was selected when the Blackfeet were at peace. This person would work with other nations. Each Blackfeet band also had a Minor Chief.

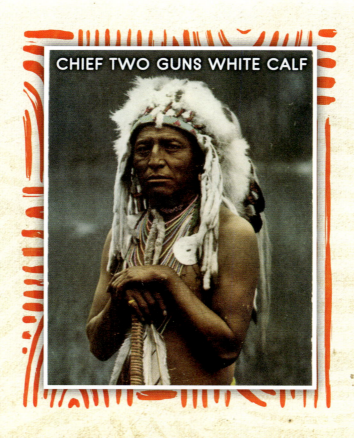
CHIEF TWO GUNS WHITE CALF

BLACKFEET WARRIORS, 1900

EUROPEAN CONTACT

Blackfeet warriors helped Blackfeet territory grow throughout the 1700s. By the 1750s, Blackfeet warriors had horses. They became even more successful. They gained important hunting grounds. The European fur trade moved into their territory by 1807. But the Blackfeet did not work with trappers until the 1830s.

ILLUSTRATION OF THE LAME BULL TREATY OF 1855

PAINTING BY CHARLES MARION RUSSELL, *WHEN BLACKFOOT AND SIOUX MEET*

The U.S. government forced the Blackfeet to sign a **treaty** in 1855. It reduced Blackfeet territory. It created the Blackfeet Indian **Reservation**. It also forced them to share hunting land with neighboring Plains Nations.

13

The Blackfeet would not give in to the U.S. government. The government knew many nations needed bison. It worked to kill all bison throughout the 1800s. Few remained by the 1880s. Because of the U.S. government's actions, the Blackfeet lost much of their culture, food, and shelter.

The Blackfeet were forced to make difficult choices. In 1895, they agreed to sell *Mistakiks*, their sacred land. It became Glacier National Park. Many people turned to farming to survive. Much of the Blackfeet Indian Reservation continues to be used for farming.

FAMOUS BLACKFOOT

ELOUISE COBELL "YELLOW BIRD WOMAN"

BIRTHDAY November 5, 1945

DEATH October 16, 2011

FAMOUS FOR One of the founders of the Native American Bank, the first bank in the U.S. owned by a Native American nation

CHIEF MOUNTAIN IN GLACIER NATIONAL PARK, A SACRED BLACKFEET SITE

BLACKFEET RANCH IN THE EARLY 1900s

TREATY 7

Blackfoot Chief Crowfoot signed Treaty 7 in 1877. This treaty created the reserves for Blackfoot people in Canada.

15

LIFE TODAY

The Blackfoot Confederacy is made up of more than 41,000 members. Many people live on the nations' reserves. Others make their homes in other parts of the United States, Canada, and the world.

Each nation of the Blackfoot Confederacy has land. Their lands were set by treaties with the U.S. and Canadian governments. The Kainai Nation is located in southern Alberta, Canada. The Piikani Nation is in southern Alberta as well. The Siksika Nation's land is just north of the Piikani and Kainai reserves. In the U.S., the Amskapi Piikani Nation's reservation is in northwest Montana.

The four nations have independent governments. The Kainai Nation, Piikani Nation, and Siksika Nation each have a Chief. Each nation also has its own **council**. The Amskapi Piikani in Montana is currently led by the Blackfeet Tribal Business Council. They may choose a Chief in the future.

Each nation's government provides public services to its members. These services include schools and health care. The nations also run businesses. The Siksika Nation runs many small businesses, including hotels and a market. The Amskapi Piikani Nation owns a casino, an art **gallery**, and more.

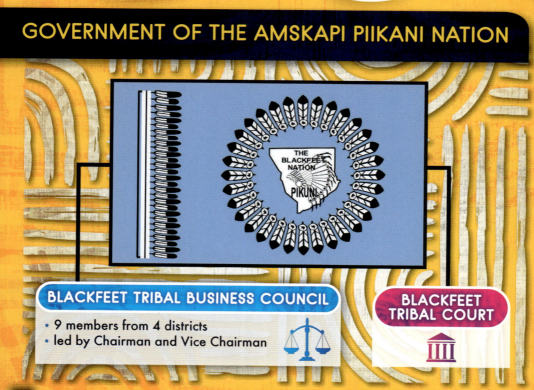

GOVERNMENT OF THE AMSKAPI PIIKANI NATION

BLACKFEET TRIBAL BUSINESS COUNCIL
- 9 members from 4 districts
- led by Chairman and Vice Chairman

BLACKFEET TRIBAL COURT

BLACKFEET HERITAGE CENTER & ART GALLERY

GLACIER PEAKS CASINO IN BROWNING, MONTANA

MAJOR BUSINESSES

Farming and ranching are common on the Blackfeet Indian Reservation. The main crops are wheat, barley, and hay.

CONTINUING TRADITIONS

NORTH AMERICAN INDIAN DAYS

Many Blackfeet people carry on the traditions that have been practiced for thousands of years. The North American Indian Days and the Siksika Nation **Pow Wow** are celebrated each year. Many people join dancing and singing contests.

Some people carry on the Blackfeet warrior tradition through horse relay races. Races are three laps of fast-paced, often bareback, riding. Riders must change horses after each lap. The races take place at events such as the Piikani Nation Indian Relay Race.

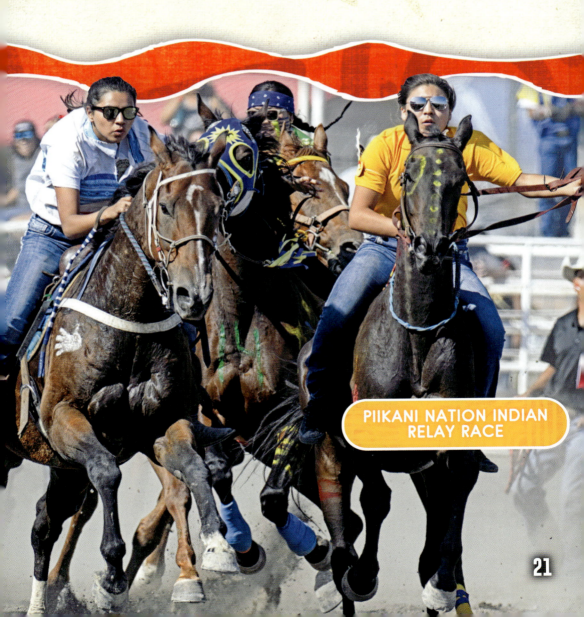

PIIKANI NATION INDIAN RELAY RACE

BISON NUMBERS

There were between 30 million and 50 million bison on the Great Plains before 1820. There were fewer than 100 wild bison by 1902.

Many Native American nations are working to grow the bison population that was destroyed in the 1800s. The Blackfeet Buffalo Program has around 700 bison. They hope that bison will one day thrive on the Blackfeet Reservation. The program also wants to release a herd into Glacier National Park and the Badger-Two Medicine area. Both places are sacred sites to the Blackfeet people.

Blackfeet artists use traditional design and cultural **inspiration** in their creations. The Lodgepole Gallery in Browning, Montana, displays works to share Blackfeet culture. The Blackfeet people work to keep their culture alive!

BLACKFEET BEADING DESIGNS

Beadwork has been an important part of Blackfeet culture for hundreds of years. Modern artists use colorful glass beads to make traditional designs.

FLOWER DESIGN

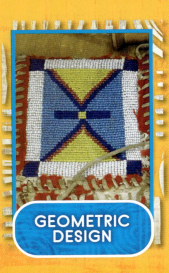

GEOMETRIC DESIGN

CURVED LINES DESIGN

FIGHT TODAY, BRIGHT TOMORROW

AN AREA IN A DROUGHT

The Blackfeet still face challenges today. They have been affected by **drought**, floods, and unsafe drinking water. These issues have damaged land and homes, caused health problems, and more.

But the Blackfeet Environmental Office is working to find solutions. Teams carry out studies. For example, they test drinking water to make sure it is safe. They make their findings public on a website. This helps people stay informed and find solutions.

BLACKFEET ENVIRONMENTAL OFFICE WEBSITE

Many people on the Blackfeet Reservation have limited access to food. Many live far from grocery stores. Food prices are also very high. A group called FAST (Food Access and **Sustainability** Team) Blackfeet works to give food to members in need. The Nation also hopes to grow and process more food on the reservation.

CATTLE RANCH

The Blackfeet work to teach people their language. The Blackfoot Language Revival group creates educational tools. Some Blackfeet members share their culture through Native America Speaks. This program is at Glacier National Park. It teaches the public about Blackfeet traditions. The Blackfeet people continue to work toward a bright future!

TIMELINE

1855
The Lame Bull Treaty establishes the Blackfeet Indian Reservation in what is now Montana

BY 1750
Horses are introduced to the Blackfeet

1865
Settlers begin moving onto Blackfeet land

1837
A smallpox outbreak in the Plains region greatly affects the Blackfeet people

1870
U.S. military members attack a band of sleeping Blackfoot people in an event known as the Blackfoot Massacre or Baker Massacre

28

1883 TO 1884
Hundreds of Blackfeet people lose their lives after millions of bison are killed throughout the mid-1800s

1987
Blackfeet National Bank, the first tribal-owned bank, opens

1877
Treaty 7 is signed by Blackfoot Chief Crowfoot of the Siksika Nation, creating reserves in Canada

1974
The Blackfeet Nation starts Blackfeet Community College

2023
Part of U.S. Highway 89 in Montana is named after Blackfeet Chief Earl Old Person

29

GLOSSARY

bands—groups of people who live as communities and share a culture

confederacy—a group of Native American nations

council—a group of people who meet to run a government

culture—the beliefs, arts, and ways of life in a place or society

drought—an extended period of time with little to no rainfall

gallery—a place where art is on display

Great Plains—a region of flat or gently rolling land in the central United States and parts of southern Canada

inspiration—something that gives someone an idea about what to do or create

Pow Wow—a Native American gathering that usually includes dancing

provinces—large areas of a country that have their own governments

reservation—land set aside by the U.S. government for the forced removal of a Native American community from their original land; reservations formed by the Canadian government are called reserves.

sacred—relating to religion

sustainability—the idea of using the land and resources in ways that will allow them to be available in the future

territory—an area of land under the control of a nation or government

traditions—the customs, ideas, or beliefs handed down from one generation to the next

treaty—an official agreement between two groups

TO LEARN MORE

AT THE LIBRARY

Bodden, Valerie. *Bison*. Mankato, Minn.: The Creative Company, 2023.

Bowman, Chris. *Glacier National Park*. Minneapolis, Minn.: Bellwether Media, 2023.

Marcks, Betty. *The Sioux*. Minneapolis, Minn.: Bellwether Media, 2024.

ON THE WEB

FACTSURFER

Factsurfer.com gives you a safe, fun way to find more information.

1. Go to www.factsurfer.com.

2. Enter "the Blackfeet" into the search box and click 🔍.

3. Select your book cover to see a list of related content.

INDEX

Amskapi Piikani Nation, 4, 16, 18
Badger-Two Medicine, 22
bands, 8, 10
beading designs, 23
bison, 6, 7, 9, 14, 22
Blackfeet Buffalo Program, 22
Blackfeet Environmental Office, 25
Blackfeet Indian Reservation, 13, 14, 16, 19, 22, 26
Blackfeet Language Revival group, 27
Blackfeet resources, 7
Chiefs, 10, 15, 18
Cobell, Elouise, 14
confederacy, 4, 16
culture, 6, 7, 14, 23, 27
drought, 24
farming, 14, 19
FAST Blackfeet, 26
foods, 6, 14, 26
future, 18, 26, 27
Glacier National Park, 14, 15, 22, 27
government of the Amskapi Piikani Nation, 18
Great Plains, 4, 22

history, 4, 6, 7, 8, 9, 10, 11, 12, 13, 14, 15, 22
homeland, 4, 5, 12, 13, 14
horses, 7, 10, 12, 21
Kainai Nation, 4, 16, 18
Lodgepole Gallery, 23
map, 5, 16
members, 16, 18, 26, 27
Mistakiks, 14
names, 4
Native America Speaks, 27
North American Indian Days, 20
Piikani Nation, 4, 16, 18, 21
Piikani Nation Indian Relay Race, 21
ranching, 15, 19, 26
reserves, 15, 16
Rocky Mountains, 4, 5
Siksika Nation, 4, 16, 18, 20
Siksika Nation Pow Wow, 20
timeline, 28–29
tipis, 9
traditions, 6, 20, 21, 23, 27
treaty, 13, 15, 16
U.S. government, 13, 14, 16
warriors, 10, 11, 12, 21

The images in this book are reproduced through the courtesy of: Eye Ubiquitous/ Alamy, front cover; kavram, pp. 3, 19 (wheat field); Pung, pp. 4-5; Stock Montage/ Getty Images, p. 6; photo-fox/ Alamy, p. 7; VladGans, p. 7 (bison); H. Armstrong Roberts/ClassicsStock/ Getty Images, p. 8; Carol Barrington/ Alamy, p. 9; Chronicle/ Alamy, p. 10; Bettmann/ Getty Images, pp. 10-11; Archive Image/ Alamy, pp. 12-13; Gustav Sohon/ Wikipedia, p. 13; Helen H. Richardson/ Getty Images, p. 14; Eric Middlekoop, p. 15 (Chief Mountain); FPG/ Getty Images, p. 15 (Blackfeet ranch); oasisamuel, p. 15 (Treaty 7); Michelle Gliders/ Alamy, pp. 16-17; Danita Delimont/ Alamy, pp. 17, 20, 22; unknown/ Wikipedia, p. 18; UrbanImages/ Alamy, p. 19 (Blackfeet Heritage Center); Pecold, p. 19 (Glacier Peaks Casino); Rick Rudnicki/ Alamy, p. 21; robertharding/ Alamy, p. 23 (flower design); Shim Harno/ Alamy, p. 23 (geometric design); Historic Images/ Alamy, p. 23 (curved line design); Prisma by Dukas Presseagentur GmbH/ Alamy, pp. 24, 31; Farknot Architect, p. 23 (website); john lambing/ Alamy, p. 25; PBH/ Alamy, p. 26; Wolfgang Kaehler/ Getty Images, p. 27; Hulton Deutsch/ Getty Images, p. 28 (1750); NurPhoto SRL/ Alamy, p. 28 (1870); James Gabbert/ Alamy, p. 29 (1877); U.S. Department of Agriculture/ Wikipedia, p. 29 (2023).